Happy Anniversary
1988
from Christopher

CAPE COD

Text by
BILL HARRIS

CRESCENT BOOKS
NEW YORK

CLB 1972
© 1988 Colour Library Books Ltd., Guildford, Surrey, England.
All rights reserved.
Printed and bound in Barcelona, Spain by Cronion, S.A.
Published 1988 by Crescent Books, distributed by Crown Publishers, Inc.
ISBN 0 517 64411 8
h g f e d c b a

Not everyone who crosses the Cape Cod Canal and heads toward the open sea out past Nauset Beach is a sun worshipper. People go down the Cape for all manner of reasons. They usually find what they're looking for: a living piece of history, the feel of the wind across the moors, high surf and even higher sand dunes, broad marshes teeming with life, brilliant sunsets across the water, moonlight reflected from hidden ponds. But what impresses everyone is something they might not notice or at least not think about until after they've gone home. It smells so wonderful out there. The tang of the salt air is what does it, some say. You're surrounded by it on Cape Cod. It's almost like being on a cruise ship. Almost, yes. But better. Because there's more to it than salt in the air.

It's the sweet smell of pine and hemlock made sweeter by the ferns at their feet and the woodbine spreading out beyond their branches in search of the sun. It's the scent of bayberry that Cape Codders have been working for generations to add to our memories of Christmas. It's the perfume of the wild roses growing everywhere you look. And it's the pungent smell of drying seaweed blended together with all the other scents, mixed well with cool, fresh air. Tangy, salt air.

Most people think of the Cape as a summer resort. Indeed, it seems as if all of Boston moves down every summer, has its phone calls forwarded and then proceeds to ignore them. But every year after Labor Day more and more of them don't bother to go back. They breathe sea air up in Boston. But it isn't Cape Cod air. Who can blame them for not wanting to go back?

Traditionally, though, Cape Cod wasn't always a place that encouraged people to stay. No one has ever been able to prove it, but it seems likely that Lief Ericsson and his Norse followers landed near Provincetown back in 1003. It seems just as likely that he established some sort of settlement there. But he went back to Norway without leaving a trace and doesn't seem to have breathed a word to anyone about the scent of bayberry.

Captain John Smith of the Virginia colony sailed past in the early 17th century. He made a map of the Cape and named it "Cape James." It's a "goodly land," he said. But he never mentioned the perfume or the soft pink and white colors of the roses that some years later Henry David Thoreau said are " ... perfectly Elysian ... an oasis in the desert."

It wasn't until 1620 that anyone came with any idea of actually living on Cape Cod, and even they sheepishly said they thought they had landed in Virginia. And they didn't actually establish farms there until 1637.

We call them Pilgrims. They called themselves Separatists. The movement that brought them to America began in 14th-century England, when John Wycliffe translated the Bible into English. It was considered heresy at the time and both Wycliffe and his English-language Bible were outlawed. By the time Elizabeth I became Queen in 1558, Catholics and Protestants were fighting over who had the true Word. The English Bible had been legalized by then, but to many it just didn't seem right that God might understand the language. Elizabeth tried to solve the problem by establishing an English Church, but some Protestants, particularly those in the North Midlands, scoffed that what she had produced was nothing more than the old Catholic Church without Latin as its official language. What was needed, they said, was a clean break with tradition and a return to the idea that the Scriptures were pure, simple truth. They argued that no man needed a priest between himself and God, no person should be involved in ritualistic worship and everyone was under an obligation to lead his life as simply as possible.

Their church was quickly outlawed, of course. Many of its followers were forced to leave their homes and moved to Holland, where religious freedom was already well-established. Those who stayed behind were eventually imprisoned by the Archbishop of York for their antisocial beliefs. It was clear they would have to leave England if they really wanted to practice what they preached.

Previous pages: sunset over Buzzard Bay, with Plymouth beyond, and (facing page) Provincetown Harbor and the Pilgrim Monument, seen from the sands near Pilgrim Lake.

America was the perfect answer. Their fellow Separatists in Holland wanted to live among their own countrymen and they were all intrigued by the idea of all those savages waiting to be converted to Christianity. But none of them had any money for such a trip. It took their leaders, William Bradford and William Brewster, three years to interest a group of London businessmen in financing an expedition for them. It was a good business investment for the Londoners, after all. These Yorkshiremen had an almost frightening work ethic and it seemed that riches would be flowing in as soon as the ship landed. But things aren't always what they seem.

They sailed from Plymouth, England, on September 6, 1620, and two months later arrived off the coast of New England. Their charter to settle in the New World had been established with the Virginia Company and, according to the agreement, they were assigned to settle at the mouth of the Hudson River. The Virginians considered it irrelevant that the Dutch had already established a colony there. When they sighted land, the captain of their ship, the *Mayflower*, obediently shifted his course southward. That's when the course of history changed.

The way the Pilgrims told it, their ship encountered dangerous shoals off the coast of Cape Cod and they decided to put ashore rather than risk being torn apart in the surf. The Cape Cod shoreline is laced with dangerous shoals and the surf in November can be fearsome. But Cape Cod Bay provided them with a haven from a lot more than the cruel sea.

The waters off New England were well charted by then, and they knew exactly where they were. They also knew that if they went any further south they'd be in territory claimed by the Virginia Company and they'd be virtual slaves of the men who had paid for their passage. And they knew that a short distance north they would come under the jurisdiction of the British Council for New England. But Cape Cod was still a no-man's land, one of the few places anywhere on the coast of North America that they could settle without any interference from the Mother Country.

They said it was God's intervention that brought them to the Cape, and who's to say it wasn't? One thing was certain, they were on their own. And, for the moment at least, out of debt. They had a debt to each other, though, and before going ashore they drew up a set of laws that would bind them together. The document, the Mayflower Compact, is one of the most important sets of laws in the history of America and became the model for other such documents that would follow in another 150 years, when their descendants decided to break their ties with the Old Country.

They stayed on the Cape for a month before finally deciding to move across the bay and, on Christmas Day, 1620, they stepped ashore on the now-famous Plymouth Rock. Most versions of American history begin their saga there. But it should be noted that the seed corn they had with them had been stolen from the Indians out at the tip of Cape Cod. It may explain why nearly 20 years passed before they ventured back to the Cape to establish its first town at Sandwich. And it may also explain why an old Cape Codder was once quoted as having said, "Plymouth Rock? Why, that's a breed of chicken, isn't it?"

By the following autumn the purloined corn had prospered and everyone in the colony was blessed with a ration of ten pounds a week. They had a community larder stocked with turkeys and ducks and venison and their grapes had produced enough wine to get them through a very long winter. They had reason to celebrate and did it in style by entertaining 90 Indians in a feast that lasted three days. It's an occasion we still celebrate with the national holiday of Thanksgiving on the fourth Thursday in November each year.

We call them the "Pilgrim Fathers" even though they were far from the first Englishmen to settle in America. And we celebrate their beginnings in Plymouth even though their first American home was on Cape Cod. History sometimes gets obscured that way. In the case of the Separatists, though, we have a more complete history than any other of the original English settlers in America. William Bradford, who arrived on the Mayflower and served as governor of the colony for the next 35 years, was an accomplished writer who kept careful records. His history wasn't published until the mid-19th century, but over the years his descendants made sure that any interested historian had access to his manuscripts. They did such a thorough job that almost no history of America gave them anything but high praise, and they undoubtedly deserved it. They thought so anyway, and before long it became an article of faith that anyone descended from one of the *Mayflower's* original passengers was a little bit better than anyone else.

There were 102 people aboard that ship, and by the middle of the 18th century they had a lot of descendants. But they were clearly a minority. By then many of their neighbors in Massachusetts were beginning to take sides over whether these colonies were, and of a right ought to be, free and independent states. The descendants of the original settlers were mostly landowners who felt things were just fine the way they were. But it seemed they couldn't go anywhere, especially the local taverns, without getting involved in an argument about it. They retaliated by forming a private club, which they called the Old Colony.

The outsiders seemed to accept the idea with good grace, which made the club's members secure enough to stage a festival they called "Forefathers' Day" which was designed to impress the world with their own importance. In December, 1769, the Old Colony rented the local tavern for a day and showed up in the afternoon dressed in costumes that had arrived on the *Mayflower*, but had long since been buried away in old trunks. The occasion was marked by an eight-course banquet. Digestion was aided by an outdoor ceremony honoring the original settlers and dedicating a rock that tradition said had been the first landing place of the Pilgrims some 150 years earlier. After the ceremonies, the members retired once again to the tavern to drink a round of toasts to their ancestors and to the King of England.

The festival was repeated each year after that and is the real basis for our present-day Thanksgiving. But for the first five years it was limited just to people who could trace their lineage back to the *Mayflower*. Then in 1774 the Sons of Liberty staged a counter-ceremony. They gathered at Plymouth Rock at sunrise on Forefathers' Day and put their backs into the task of stealing it. Their intention was to move it to the center of the town Common, where they planned to use it as the anchor for a Liberty Pole, the symbol of the gathering revolution.

But before they could move it, the rock split into two parts. The members of the Old Colony were horrified, but the Sons of Liberty considered it a good omen, indicating that that Britain would soon be separated from her colonies in the same way. Besides, it was easier to move half the rock than the whole thing, and leaving the other half where it had been still marked the old Pilgrim landing spot. Still, it took 20 oxen to move the piece that went to the Common, where it stayed for the next 60 years before being taken back to the harbor to be used as a paving stone. The two halves were finally cemented back together in 1880.

By then Thanksgiving was already an American institution, and every year school children across the country were dressing up in Indian warpaint or tall black hats to commemorate the settlers' first winter looking out over Cape Cod. And about the same time the Cape began making an important contribution to America's Thanksgiving dinners. It was when wild cranberries were tamed for the first time and became the Cape's most important export, not to mention a staple as important to a Thanksgiving feast as the turkey itself.

Cranberry vines thrive in the bogs on the Cape and the islands that surround it. The combination of rich peat and sand provides an environment not found anywhere else. The plant takes its name from the tiny pink flowers it produces. People with sharp eyes and vivid imaginations say the blossoms look like the head and neck of a crane, and years ago they called the vine a craneberry. In early summer, when the plants are in bloom and the bogs heavy with their fragrance, bees seem to come from all over Massachusetts to nuzzle in them. When they've moved enough pollen around, the heavy green berries begin to form, almost, it seems, before the blossoms have fallen off. The flowers seem too small for such big plants, but the berries that follow them seem too big for such fragile plants. Somehow it all works, though, and by early fall the green has turned to red and they'll be harvested in much the same way they were gathered back when only the Indians knew about these tart-sweet berries.

Harvesters use a wooden scoop with comb-like teeth up front. As they comb through the vines the tool, made of hard maple, picks up wax from the leaves and in no time at all is polished to a high gloss, which is one reason why they're so prized as souvenirs in the local gift shops. But the best souvenir any visitor can have is the memory of watching a cranberry harvest and seeing the pickers' arms describe huge arcs in the air as they move from one vine to the next on their knees, filling their bags with the crimson berries.

When they've finished and the berries are packed in weathered gray boxes at the edge of the bogs, it would seem as though the show might be over for another year. But the best is yet to come. The first frost turns the leaves a vivid shade of purple and the cranberry vines become the stars of the annual show of fall foliage. But their part in the show is over quickly. Not long after the leaves begin to change their color, the bogs are flooded to protect the plants over the winter. After that, summer visitors wouldn't recognize the Cape. What look from a distance like fields the rest of the year become still ponds in the winter, reflecting the blue of the sky and adding a sparkle to the landscape. From up close the plants the water is protecting still have their purple leaves, which gives the ponds a special color.

The colors of the Cape are as delightful as its scents, especially in the fall. The sandy soil is the color of straw, the landscape dotted with silver-gray trees and rough grass. The houses are sheathed in cedar that turns a rich and pleasing shade of gray and picks up accents of muted green moss. There is a barrenness there, to be sure, but also thick forests and marshes, and sand dunes covered with protective grasses and plants. The autumn landscape, wrote Thoreau, "was like the richest rug imaginable ... no damask nor velvet, nor Tyrian dye or stuffs, nor the work of any loom could ever match it. There was the incredibly bright red of the huckleberry and the reddish brown of the bayberry mixed with the bright and living green of the pitch-pine. ... Coming from the country as I did, and many autumnal woods as I had seen, this was the most novel and remarkable sight that I saw on the Cape."

The people who live year 'round in the 15 towns on the Cape smilingly attest to his assessment every year when they read about traffic jams in the Berkshires caused by tourists the natives up there call "leaf peepers." They know that the show is better on Cape Cod and that the traffic jams on Route 6 usually disappear after Labor Day when the population dwindles back to a manageable size. After the first weekend in September, in spite of the fact that Cape Cod winters are milder than in the rest of Massachusetts and the fall is possibly more beautiful, vacationers head south for warmer beaches, west for what they've been told are prettier displays of fall color, and north for a bit of skiing. The natives don't care. They know the best is coming, and though they don't mind sharing it, there is pleasure in solitude after all, and nowhere on the East Coast of the United States is solitude as much of a pleasure as it is on old Cape Cod.

Facing page: an aerial view of Edgartown and the tip of Chappaquiddick Island.

At the tip of the great, sandy curve of Cape Cod are the Province Lands and Provincetown, where the Pilgrims first landed in the New World. South of here the land continues to curl round, like the tail of a scorpion, thinning to a mere thread of sand at Wood End (previous pages) and ending at Long Point, once a fishing community. The economy of Provincetown is still based on fishing and its fleet is manned largely by the Portuguese descendants of sailors who arrived here during the whaling days of the 1800s. This, as well as its 18th-century architecture, gives the town a strong sense of continuity with the past. Since the 1920s, however, Provincetown, like the whole of the Cape, has undergone one major change – the influx of the rich and fashionable and today, glamorous pleasure craft ripple the same Provincetown Harbor waters (these pages) that reflect fishing boats and bobbing trawlers.

13

It is due largely to Provincetown's sizeable, sheltered harbor that the town is still a successful fishing port when many other Cape Cod communities have long since seen their fleets come in for the last time. Maritime activity in Provincetown (these pages) centers around MacMillan Wharf (previous pages and left), where, each year, millions of pounds of fish are landed. While fishing is a year-round pursuit, vacationing is not, and life in Provincetown changes dramatically with the seasons. In the summer the town comes alive with people sunbathing, swimming and sailing, and demand for seaside properties, from balconied mansions to beach huts, is extremely high. Below: uninterrupted views of the sea are afforded by this isolated Coast Guard Station, idyllically situated on the golden sand dunes at Race Point.

Scenes of the Province Lands' wind-sculpted sands (right), seagulls circling fishing boats and white clapboard against blue sky have attracted artists to Provincetown (remaining pictures and overleaf) for decades. Its quiet, romantic beauty and peacefulness have also provided ideal conditions for many writers, such as Eugene O'Neill, whose early plays were often produced here at a small, wharf-side theater. Looking at boats in Provincetown Harbor (overleaf left) is a favorite pastime of tourists and residents alike. There are sleek, white-sailed schooners gliding quietly through the waters while moored fishing boats with clattering rigging bob together, filled with all kinds of interesting paraphernalia. Right: a view of Provincetown from across the harbor, its skyline silhouetted against hazy dawn light and dominated by the Pilgrim Monument.

Previous pages and overleaf: Provincetown and its harbor below the Pilgrim Monument. Built on the summit of a 100-foot-high hill, this imposing, 252-foot-high tower can be seen for miles around, soaring above the flat countryside. The monument was erected between 1907 and 1910 and commemorates the landing of the Pilgrims in 1620. Although it is composed of granite from Maine, the writer Josef Berger noted with some irony that "it is thoroughly American in its makeup ... the designer is Italian; the plans were made by an army engineer of French and Swiss descent; it was built by the Irish and is taken care of by Portuguese; and annually is climbed by several thousand *Mayflower* descendants." Facing page top: Race Point, the westernmost tip of the Cape and part of the everchanging sand-dune landscape of the Province Lands.

25

This page: clapboard buildings in Provincetown, and (facing page) the Highland Light, which, built in 1797, is the oldest lighthouse on Cape Cod and is situated on a stretch of land between Pilgrim Heights and Truro. Overleaf: Provincetown seen from the Pilgrim Monument.

Previous pages left: Provincetown beachfront and the Pilgrim Monument and (previous pages right and overleaf) the great curve of the Province Lands and Provincetown Harbor. Facing page: Herring Cove Beach, which lies along the western edge of the Province Lands, and (below) Race Point, part of the Provincetown dunes (left). These dunes lie within the 27,000-acre stretch of Cape Cod National Seashore, which was established in 1961 and is one of the last great expanses of uninterrupted wilderness along the Atlantic coast. Following pages: sunset over Provincetown.

Previous pages: the beachfront at Provincetown and (this page) the Coast Guard Station at Race Point (facing page top), where pale green marram grass somehow thrives on the wind-blown sands. Facing page bottom and overleaf left bottom sunset over the waters of Cape Cod Bay at Pond Village Beach, North Truro. Overleaf: (left top) fishing on Provincetown dunes, (right bottom) Head of the Meadow Beach, Truro and (right top) the beach at Corn Hill, Truro. It was on this hill, two days after their landing in 1620, that a party of Pilgrims came across a cache of Indian corn seed. The seed they took from here enabled them to start arable farming, and probably saved them from starvation.

42

Soon after Truro (these pages) received town status in 1709, its inhabitants built their first Congregational Church (facing page) on the windy Hill of Storms. Top: Bay Village Road in North Truro, (above) Head of the Meadow Beach and (right) the nearby Highland Light.

North of Truro, at Wellfleet, two of the most popular attractions of Cape Cod National Seashore are to be found – the site of the Marconi wireless station and spectacular Marconi Beach (previous pages, these pages and overleaf left top). By 1901, Guglielmo Marconi, the Italian inventor of wireless telegraphy, had already sent signals across the English Channel and was ready to attempt a trans-Atlantic transmission. He decided that the message would be sent from Wellfleet, as it had a clear path to England, but what he didn't know was that high winds were common in this area, and gales blew down his first radio station, the remains of which can still be seen (overleaf left bottom). His second was stronger and made the first trans-Atlantic transmission on 18 January 1903. The station is now gone, but in its place, recalling the event, is an interpretation center (overleaf right bottom) and a commemorative statue of Marconi (overleaf right top).

The Highland Light (previous pages), in North Truro, is one of the most powerful beacons on the Atlantic coast and can be seen over 20 miles away. As one of the earliest lights it had humble beginnings, the first structure on the site having been powered by 24 whale oil lamps with reflectors. Above: sand-dunes in Cape Cod National Seashore, and (remaining pictures) views around Eastham, one of the towns included in the area known as "Nawsett," which was annexed to the Plymouth Colony in 1640 following a patent from the Earl of Warwick. Facing page: Penniman House and its whalebone gateway, built in 1876 by whaling captain Edward Penniman, and (left) the silver sands of Coast Guard Beach. Overleaf: (left) the Eastham Windmill, built around 1680, and (right) one of the most historic walks in the Eastham environs, the Fort Hill swamp trail, which passes old homesites, orchards, and salt works all dating from the pioneer days.

Dramatic in its history and its beauty, Nauset Light Beach (previous pages) at Eastham (these pages), has seen several shipwrecks. According to legend, however, many of these were due to the villainous practice of "mooncussing," or luring ships aground by waving with lanterns on moonless nights for the purpose of "salvaging" the booty. This legend is supported by the fact that a man called Collins met with "obstinate resistance" to the idea of building a lighthouse on the beach. His plans were eventually realized in 1838, when he became the keeper of a group of three lights known as the "three sisters." Today, a strong steel tower stands in their place (left), moved there in 1923 from Chatham. Below: an informative plaque at the Coast Guard Beach Center (facing page), on Coast Guard Beach, which includes a museum recalling the work of the earliest coast guards. Overleaf: Nauset Light Beach and Nauset Lighthouse.

Above: a fresh water pond on Nauset Beach, near Nauset Harbor, part of Orleans' serene waterfront (these pages). As the Cape's second smallest town, Orleans seems to have a surprisingly large share of waterfront. Its western shoreline, Shaket Beach, is washed by the waters of Cape Cod Bay, while its northern, eastern and southern reaches are bordered by Town Cove, Nauset Harbor and Pleasant Bay, which has myriad calm bays and inlets where small boats are moored. Overleaf: a typical seascape on Cape Cod National Seashore – uninterrupted stretches of blue sea and sky, golden sand and the soft colors of grass on the dunes.

At the southeastern "corner" of the Cape is the town of Chatham, famous for its fogs and shipwrecks and saved from indiscriminate commercialism by strict zoning laws. Right: the harbor of Chathamport, and (below) the leafy, unspoiled village of Chatham. Facing page: (top) Chatham Lighthouse, and (bottom) an inviting stretch of sand and sea at Orleans.

Previous pages: Wychmere Harbor in Harwichport, one of the six charming villages in the town of Harwich (these pages and overleaf). This popular resort area, washed by the warm waters of Nantucket Sound, no longer has a thriving fishing industry, but is still the major center for the Cape's main agricultural asset – cranberries. Harwich's terrain of shallow ponds and marshlands (above, facing page bottom and overleaf) is ideal for the cultivation of these sharp, red berries, which were once known as "crane berries" and were left for the birds to eat.

Facing page and left: calm harbor waters and (below) a sandy beach in Harwich. By the mid-1700s relations between the South and North Parishes of Harwich had become less than friendly, and the inhabitants of the latter began to want independence from the original settlement. Thus, in 1803 they incorporated the town of Brewster, naming it after Elder William Brewster. By 1880 this proud community decided to build itself a new Town Hall and a grand, Queen Anne-style mansion (overleaf right), was erected at considerable cost. It now houses the Brewster Historical Society Museum. Another of the town's attractions is Nickerson State Park, named for the Brewster entrepreneur Roland C. Nickerson. Covering 1,750 acres, the park contains a beautiful forest, three trout-stocked ponds and the lovely Cliff Pond (overleaf left), which is actually a 204-acre lake.

Previous pages: an aerial view over Cobbs Pond and the smaller Myricks Pond, by the beach between West Brewster and East Brewster. Facing page and below: isolated marshlands and beaches at Brewster, which provide an ideal habitat for many types of seabirds, and (left) Brewster's famous old Stoney Brook Mill, which was built in 1873 to replace the original, water-powered grist mill built by Thomas Prence in 1663. It is the last of several mills and businesses once in the area, which included industries as diverse as weaving, spinning, tanning and shoemaking. Overleaf: low tide reveals the patterned sands of Cape Cod Bay near Brewster.

Since 1700 there have been houses of worship on the site of the First Parish Church of Brewster (previous pages left), which dates from 1834. Thus its cemetery is of great historical interest, containing memorials to many of Brewster's old sea captians, most of whom were lost at sea. Previous pages right: 18th-century Smock Windmill, which was built in 1795 and ground corn until around 1900. Right: one of the beaches of Dennis, a charming cranberry-growing town comprised of five villages. West Dennis and South Dennis are separated from neighboring Yarmouth by the Bass River (remaining pictures), which is spanned by the Bass River Bridge.

The mid-Cape town of Yarmouth, with its golden marshland (below) and quiet backwaters (left), is one of the most popular retirement towns on the Cape and is enjoying a rapid population boom. Tourists are drawn by its convenient mid-Cape location, a sunny south coast and many historical treasures, including the Church of the New Jerusalem (facing page) in Yarmouth Port. Also known as the Swedenborgian Church, its members belong to a small sect which derives its beliefs from interpretations of the scriptures by Emanuel Swedenborg, a Swedish scientist and mystic of the early 18th century. The attractive church was built in 1870 by an Italian architect and differs quite considerably from other Cape churches of its time.

Previous pages: (right) the First Congregational Church, built in 1870, (left top) the fine colonial mansion of Winslow Crocker House, built in 1780, both in Yarmouth Port, and (left bottom) houses on a rocky promontory near Yarmouth. In the southwest corner of Barnstable, on Nantucket Sound, stands Hyannis, the main commercial center of the Cape's tourist industry. Among its attractions are picturesque Hyannis Harbor (above and overleaf), with its lighthouse (facing page bottom), and the fashionable village of Hyannisport (facing page top). The Kennedy family's summer home is located here, and in 1966 the village proudly opened its J.F.K. Memorial (left), which features a medallion of the late president.

Right: the Kennedy family home seen from Hyannisport Golf Course on Sunset Hill. Hyannisport is only one of the ten villages that constitute Barnstable, the Cape's largest town. Once the county seat for a large region that included Plymouth and the Bristol Counties, Barnstable was the meeting place for literally thousands of 18th-century colonists who opposed the King's authority. They convened in the Colonial Court House (facing page), which was built in 1774 and is now a museum exhibiting Bicentennial memorabilia. On the side of the town washed by Cape Cod Bay lies Barnstable Harbor (below), into which flows marshy Maraspin Creek (overleaf).

As the oldest town on Cape Cod, Sandwich (these pages) is both beautiful to look at and rich in historical attractions. The Dexter Grist Mill (facing page top) was built during the mid-17th century, when a certain Thomas Dexter was asked by the town to "go on to build the mill new againe," while Hoxie House (left) allegedly dates from 1637 and is the oldest house on the Cape. It has a typical 17th-century salt box structure, small leaded windows and authentic furniture on loan from the Boston Museum of Fine Arts. Remaining pictures: a boardwalk leading through silky grasslands to a beach at Sandwich. Overleaf: Mill Creek Marsh, backed by the spires of Sandwich.

Falmouth, a large town on the elbow of Cape Cod, is washed by the waters of Vineyard Sound to the south and Buzzards Bay to the east. Like many Cape towns it was named after an English seaport, although it was known by the Indian name of Succonessitt in 1660. It was then that Isaac Robinson arrived with a group of non-conformists, largely Congregationalists, who wanted independence from the intolerant church-state of Massachusetts. The settlement also attracted many Quakers, meeting houses were built and the town flourished and was renamed Falmouth in 1693. Below: Megansett Harbor in North Falmouth, (facing page top) Falmouth Harbor on Vineyard Sound and (right) boats moored on an inlet (facing page bottom and overleaf) near West Falmouth.

At the extreme southwestern corner of Falmouth, on the "funny bone" of the Cape's elbow, is Woods Hole (these pages), which was once a major whaling port. Its two great harbors and myriad bays and inlets still shelter yachts, fishing boats and ferries, but the village's economy now relies mainly on its scientific community, for the establishment of Woods Hole Oceanographic Institution, the Marine Biological Laboratory and the National Marine Fisheries Service have made it one of the largest centers for marine research in the world.

Lying five miles off the southern coast of Cape Cod, Martha's Vineyard (these pages) is New England's largest island. Its land mass of nearly one hundred square miles was separated from the mainland by rising seas between three and four thousand years ago. Since then the Atlantic has eaten away at the coastline to create a rugged shoreline, as well as building sandy barrier beaches that form tranquil ponds and inlets. Were it not for two small barrier beaches, Nashaquitsa, with its lovely Nashaquitsa Cliffs (facing page and below), at the west end of the Vineyard, would almost be an island. Wilder and less developed than the eastern reaches, the island's western tip ends at Gay Head, where a lonely lighthouse (left and overleaf) stands strong against relentless winds.

Being an island, Martha's Vineyard (these pages and overleaf) has retained much of its original character and is quite distinct from the Cape. It was named in 1602 by the English explorer Bartholomew Gosnold, who was struck by the abundance of wild grapes and named this island "Vineyard" after his little daughter Martha. Gosnold only stayed for one summer, but the name was retained by the first English settlers who arrived in 1641. They were led by the son of Thomas Mayhew, who bought the Vineyard, together with Nantucket and the Elizabeth Islands, for the absurd sum of 40 pounds. That Mayhews still live on the island testifies to its sense of continuity with the past. Life in the little village of Menemsha, to the west, still revolves around its salty, bustling harbor (below and overleaf), while the farm (right) near Lambert Cove in West Tisbury has been breeding horses for decades.

Previous pages: Edgartown, the county seat and the Vineyard's center for business, administration and culture. The first settlement on the Vineyard and later a prosperous whaling port, Edgartown is also steeped in history and rich in interesting buildings, including the Federated Church (facing page), which was built in 1828 and unites Baptists and Congregationalists. Oak Bluffs (above) was originally named Cottage City when it broke away from Edgartown in 1880 to become a separate town. It is famous as the site of the Methodist Camp Meeting, at which, in the 1860s, worshippers began replacing their tents with ornate "gingerbread cottages." Left: a horse farm near Lambert Cove, West Tisbury, and (overleaf) Menemsha Harbor.

Previous pages: (left) Edgartown Harbor, part of its downtown area and Lighthouse Beach, the site of Edgartown Lighthouse (facing page), and (right) Chappaquiddick's Cape Poge Bay and the Jeep Trail on its sandy eastern border, which leads past grassy Little Neck and the almost-circular Shear Pen Pond to Cape Poge and its lighthouse, all on Martha's Vineyard. From Edgartown's docks the little *On Time* ferry (right) leaves for Chappaquiddick – as it has no schedule for this three-minute journey it is always "on time." Above: Dyke Bridge on Chappaquiddick Island. Overleaf: Edgartown.

130

Maybe because it lies much further away from the Cape than Martha's Vineyard, Nantucket has a lonelier, more rural atmosphere than its sister island. Tourism has not spoiled it, and development has tended to blend in with the environment rather than mar it. Facing page: (top) Atlantic breezes buffet the sturdy lighthouse and roll across the hilly moors at Sankaty Head and (bottom) houses in Nantucket Harbor make a harmonious picture of weathered, gray clapboarding and rippled waters. Among Nantucket's many historic attractions is the Dutch-style Old Mill (left), which dates from 1746 and was built by Nathan Wilbur with wood salvaged from shipwrecks, and the island's oldest structure, the Jethro Coffin House of 1686, where a charming kitchen (below) displays a selection of period furniture and utensils. Overleaf: an aerial view of Edgartown.

Brant Point Lighthouse (right) guards the entrance to the harbor of Nantucket, the second major island off the southern coast of Cape Cod. Like Edgartown, the town of Nantucket (remaining pictures) thrived as a whaling port in the 18th century and boasts many fine mansions from that period.

One of the most opulent of the old houses in Nantucket town is the Hadwen House (right), built in 1823 by William Hadwen. A silversmith from Newport, Rhode Island, he probably fashioned the house after Newport's luxurious mansions. The "keeping room" (below) belongs to the simpler, but no less attractive 1800 House, which served as the home of the High Sheriff of Nantucket County. It contains many interesting exhibits, including a Chippendale-style chair thrown from the Nantucket ship *Beaver* at the Boston Tea Party. Facing page: (top) the Job Macy House of 1750 on New Dollar Lane, and (bottom) the beautifully-fitted keeping room of the Nathaniel Macy House, which was built in Sherborne during the early 18th century and moved to its present location in 1741.

Facing page: (top and bottom left) the calm waters of Nantucket Harbor, and (bottom right) clapboard houses in Nantucket town. Above: the drawing room and (left) a bedroom in the opulent Hadwen House, which is also known as the Satler Memorial as it was given to the Nantucket Historical Association by the former Jean Satler in commemoration of her family. The beautiful furniture, fine paintings and exquisite china and glassware in the house indicate the wealth that many Nantucketers enjoyed during the town's great whaling days. Overleaf: the waters of Nantucket, beyond sandy Dionis Beach, at the western end of Nantucket Island.